Spelling for Kids

An Interactive Vocabulary & Spelling Workbook for 5 - 6 Year-Olds.

(With AudioBook Lessons)

By
Bukky Ekine-Ogunlana

Spelling One

An Interactive Vocabulary & Spelling Workbook for 5 Year Olds.

www.tcecpublishing.com

© Copyright Bukky Ekine-Ogunlana 2024 - All rights reserved.

The content of this book may not be reproduced, duplicated, or transmitted without direct written permission from the author or the publisher. Under no circumstance will any blame or legal responsibility be held against the publisher, or author, for any damages, reparation, or monetary loss due to the information contained within this book. Either directly or indirectly. You are responsible for your own choices, actions, and results.

Legal Notice:

This book is copyright protected. This book is only for personal use. You cannot amend, distribute, sell, use, quote, or paraphrase any part, or the content within this book, without the consent of the author or publisher.

Disclaimer Notice:

Please note the information contained within this document is for educational and entertainment purposes only. All effort has been executed to present accurate, up-to-date, reliable, and complete information. No warranties of any kind are declared or implied. Readers acknowledge that the author is not engaging in the rendering of legal, financial, medical, or professional advice. The content within this book has been derived from various sources. Please consult a licensed professional before attempting any techniques outlined in this book.

By reading this document, the reader agrees that under no circumstances is the author responsible for any direct or indirect losses incurred as a result of the use of the information contained within this document, including, but not limited to, errors, omissions, or inaccuracies.

Published by
TCEC Publishing

Table of Contents

Dedication..8
Introduction..9

Spelling 1-1 10
Spelling 1-2 14
Spelling 1-3 16
Spelling 1-4 22
Spelling 1-5 26
Spelling 1-6 30
Spelling 1-7 34
Spelling 1-8 38
Spelling 1-9 42
Spelling 1-10 46
Spelling 1-11 50
Spelling 1-12 54
Spelling 1-13 58
Spelling 1-14 62
Spelling 1-15 66
Spelling 1-16 70
Spelling 1-17 74
Spelling 1-18 78
Spelling 1-19 82
Spelling 1-20 86

Conclusion..90

Table of Contents

Spelling Two 91

Spelling 2-1 93
Spelling 2-2 97
Spelling 2-3 101
Spelling 2-4 105
Spelling 2-5 109
Spelling 2-6 113
Spelling 2-7 117
Spelling 2-8 121
Spelling 2-9 125
Spelling 2-10 129
Spelling 2-11 133
Spelling 2-12 137
Spelling 2-13 141
Spelling 2-14 145
Spelling 2-15 149
Spelling 2-16 153
Spelling 2-17 157
Spelling 2-18 161
Spelling 2-19 165
Spelling 2-20 169

Table of Contents

Spelling 2-21 173
Spelling 2-22 177

Review 181
Conclusion 182
Spelling 1 Answers 183
Spelling 2 Answers 184
Other Books You Love 204
Spelling 1 Audiobook 208
Spelling 2 Audiobook 209
Facebook Community 210
References 212

Dedication

This book is dedicated to our three exceptional children and all the beautiful children worldwide who have passed through the T.C.E.C 6-16 years program over the years. Thank you for the opportunity to serve you and invest in your colorful and bright future.

Introduction

Welcome to the first book of the Spelling for Kids series! This book will introduce you to practicing your spelling while enjoying it too!
It is ideal for 5-year-olds.

In Spelling One, you will learn 240 words and add them to your vocabulary. These are easy, everyday, high-frequency words we all use. Therefore, you should learn to write them down and recognise them in a sentence.

You will hear each word from the audiobook, see it written in a sentence and then write it down yourself (no cheating) to practice its dictation. Of course, you can always go back to the words you struggle with and repeat the exercise for them separately or repeat the whole chapter if necessary.

So, are you ready to thrive in spelling?

Let's begin!

Spelling 1-1

1. Spell:

I will give you _____ sticker if you finish your work.

2. Spell:

_____ you want a choco cookie?

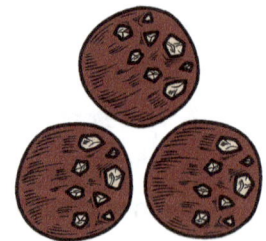

3. Spell:

Happy birthday _____ you!

Spelling 1-1

4. Spell:
Which _____ the two is correct?

5. Spell:
Who _____ I can't do it alone?

6. Spell:
Will you _____ my friend?

Spelling 1-1

7. Spell:
Can you do _____
a favor, please?

8. Spell:
My sister is _____
year old.

9. Spell:
Do you have _____
money for ice cream?

Spelling 1-1

10. Spell:

On your marks. Get set

_____!

11. Spell:

She went to the garden

_____ she could

play.

12. Spell:

John broke the glass

_____ accident.

That's it for lesson 1…Great work!

Spelling 1-2

1. Spell:

Jake likes fish

_____ chips.

2. Spell:

Jude likes _____ lollies.

3. Spell:

The _____ saves food all summer to have for the winter.

spelling 1-2

4. Spell:

Drinking _____ chocolate

makes me calm.

5. Spell:

John will have done his homework

_____ noon.

6. Spell:

_____ on your

coat, Mary; It's cold outside.

Spelling 1-2

7. Spell:

Tigers can _____ very fast.

8. Spell:

Jude wants to be _____ a game show.

9. Spell:

_____ you see the butterfly that came through the window?

Spelling 1-2

10. Spell:

It's a _____ !!
Congratulations on your newborn
baby.

11. Spell:

_____ my point of
view, what David did was wrong.

12. Spell:

The baby is sleeping in the
_____.

Congrats! You have finished learning the words in lesson 2. Remember to use your dictionary to find the meaning of all the new words you have learned.

Spelling 1-3

1. Spell:
You _____ a brave boy Adam.

2. Spell:
I went inside the house and _____ that big dog in the yard.

3. Spell:
Do _____ like vanilla ice cream?

Spelling 1-3

4. Spell:

_____ , I like chocolate cake.

5. Spell:

The school _____ arrives every day at 7:30.

6. Spell:

_____ teacher was kind to my sister.

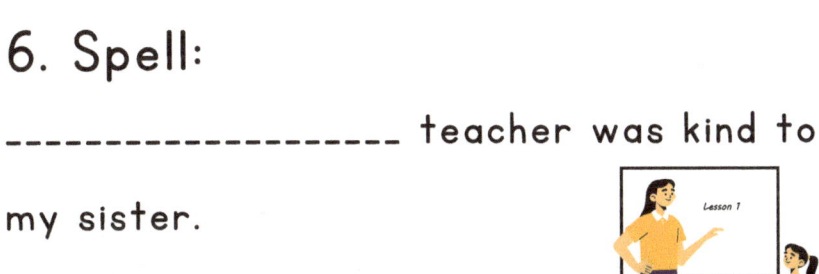

Spelling 1-3

7. Spell:

I _____ for the bus in the morning.

8. Spell:

Please _____ here and wait for me.

9. Spell:

I am allergic to _____.

Spelling 1-3

10. Spell:

I had a _____ of

tea with my breakfast.

11. Spell:

It is _____ birthday today.

12. Spell:

Great_____, Tom! I am

proud of you!

You've made it! You completed lesson 3. Pay attention, kids; if you find it difficult to learn some words, you should write them down on paper. That will help you remember them better.

Spelling 1-4

1. Spell:

The _____ of England is white and red.

2. Spell:

_____ is more clever than Mike.

3. Spell:

_____ prefer pancakes for breakfast.

spelling 1-4

4. Spell:
Sam hit his right _____ and could not play in the football game.

5. Spell:
Amelia likes to stroke the _____.

6. Spell:
Going to the fairground is always _____.

Spelling 1-4

7. Spell:

Mathew kept his toys in the

_____ bag.

8. Spell:

_____, I will never tell you

a lie.

9. Spell:

Jack likes _____

because he is a good player.

Spelling 1-4

10. Spell:
It was _____ older sister that taught me how to make pizza.

11. Spell:
Come on, dad; can you take _____, for pizza tonight?

12. Spell:
_____ has long blonde hair.

Great! Lesson 4 is over! I suggest you get some rest before going on to the next lesson. That will help you recharge and return to the next task more refreshed! Great work!

Spelling 1-5

1. Spell:

My _____ is taller than my mum.

2. Spell:

Reading a _____ is the best company.

3. Spell:

Climbing a _____ can be dangerous.

Spelling 1-5

4. Spell:

_____, fast and don't look back!

5. Spell:

I _____ to the cinema on Saturday to watch a film.

6. Spell:

_____, I can do my work myself.

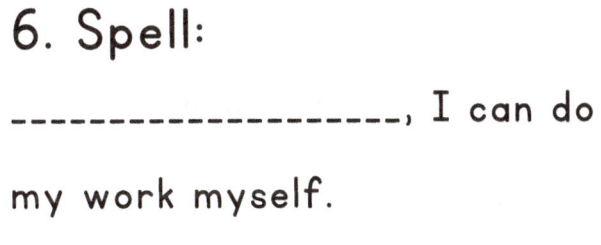

Spelling 1-5

7. Spell:

I cannot study_____ all that noise outside.

8. Spell:

_____ sister is five years old.

9. Spell:

The _____ constantly barks at the cat when he sees it.

Spelling 1-5

10. Spell:

I bought my crayon _____ the lesson.

11. Spell:

He broke the _____ of the stool.

12. Spell:

A _____ should always honor his word.

Fantastic! You have finished the words in lesson 5. What a task! Kids, keep a note: An easy way to learn the majority of new words is to break them apart; in that way, the words can be easily organized from the shortest to the longest.

Spelling 1-6

1. Spell:

_____ favorite movie is The Beauty and the Beast.

2. Spell:

_____the teacher politely, and she will answer your question.

3. Spell:

Have you _____ your clothes in the laundry?

Spelling 1-6

4. Spell:

Who _____ Jude's music teacher?

5. Spell:

_____ it my turn to wash the dishes, Tom?

6. Spell:

David _____ two sisters.

Spelling 1-6

7. Spell:

_____ are a friendly

person.

8. Spell:

He only _____

he was sorry, and he left.

9. Spell:

It was _____fault

that the parrot left the cage.

Spelling 1-6

10. Spell:

_____ are coming to my

party on Sunday.

11. Spell:

Where _____ you

yesterday?

12. Spell:

_____ is my

graduation day!

Lesson 6 has come to an end. Awesome! Keep up the excellent work! And do not forget: Repetition makes the master!

Spelling 1-7

1. Spell:

I will_____ the

sack race if I practice.

2. Spell:

Helen _____ two

brothers and a sister.

3. Spell:

There is only one _____

in my team.

spelling 1-7

4. Spell:

_____ like to watch Tom

and Jerry on Disney+.

5. Spell:

_____ morning to all

of you!

6. Spell:

A cry for _____ was

heard from down the road.

Spelling 1-7

7. Spell:
I will invite _____ of my friends to my beach party.

8. Spell:
The kitchen _____ is new.

9. Spell:
_____ you have any pokémon stickers?

Spelling 1-7

10. Spell:

I felt really _____ when my friend moved away from my street.

11. Spell:

Lilian wore a pretty _____ for her birthday party.

12. Spell:

A _____ is the best company for a child.

Look at how far you have gone! You have reached and completed lesson 7. What a student you are! Congratulations!

Spelling 1-8

1. Spell:

The pig likes staying in the

_____.

2. Spell:

The farmer sold cow's _____

to the market.

3. Spell:

I am wearing a _____

dress to Lucy's party.

Spelling 1-8

4. Spell:

_____ Red Riding Hood went through the forest to visit her grandmother.

5. Spell:

Breakfast will be served _____ 8:00 am.

6. Spell:

_____ Lion King used to be one of my favorite movies.

Spelling 1-8

7. Spell:

Can you _____ me

a cup of cold water, please?

8. Spell:

Felix did _____

over the fence.

9. Spell:

My mum did _____

me on the back for being good.

spelling 1-8

10. Spell:
The _____ flew over my house.

11. Spell:
Mom sings a lullaby to the _____ before taking her to bed.

12. Spell:
I _____ ice cream.

Look at you! You are natural! And it seems that you will be a spelling bee master pretty soon! You have just finished lesson 8.

Spelling 1-9

1. Spell:

In the zoo, you can also see some

_____ animals.

2. Spell:

_____ of my friends are

coming to my party.

3. Spell:

_____ of my parents are

kind to me.

Spelling 1-9

4. Spell:

Let the _____ come

to me, said Jesus.

5. Spell:

I can _____ the apple

tree.

6. Spell:

I _____ wish he

could come to my birthday party.

Spelling 1-9

7. Spell:

How_____ are you?

8. Spell:

_____ people came to my birthday party.

9. Spell:

My _____ are in my cupboard.

spelling 1-9

10. Spell:

It's _____ outside. Why don't we light up the fireplace?

11. Spell:

_____ is the most precious material on earth.

12. Spell:

I can _____ a ball for ten minutes without it dropping.

Well done! You have finished lesson 9. You should be proud of yourself! And remember this: Always enunciate each word properly; this method will help you spell the word correctly.

Spelling 1-10

1. Spell:

Ella walked _____

her classroom.

2. Spell:

My _____ is a

police officer.

3. Spell:

I am the best student in my

_____.

Spelling 1-10

4. Spell:
Without _____, there is no life.

5. Spell:
You have to repeat the lesson _____ to remember it.

6. Spell:
Cows eat _____.

spelling 1-10

7. Spell:

Freddy did _____

the ball on time to Felix.

8. Spell:

Angela pulled the _____

from the soil.

9. Spell:

This _____ leads to

the hidden treasure.

Spelling 1-10

10. Spell:

Elizabeth had a _____

in the morning.

11. Spell:

An _____ is sixty

minutes.

12. Spell:

Please _____ your car from

here, because parking

is not allowed.

You completed lesson 10! Bravo! You are doing a great job. Pretty soon, you will be an expert in spelling.

Spelling 1-11

1. Spell:

Oliver was able to _____ that the teacher was right.

2. Spell:

Nina shared _____ of her sausage roll with Tina.

3. Spell:

_____ is bad for the teeth.

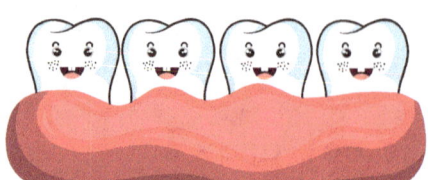

Spelling 1-11

4. Spell:

_____ you come with me to the doctor's.

5. Spell:

_____ you like cream with your coffee?

6. Spell:
Eve is not _____ if she will attend the piano lesson.

Spelling 1-11

7. Spell:
Cameron had an operation on his right _____

8. Spell:
You _____ always carry a painkiller with you.

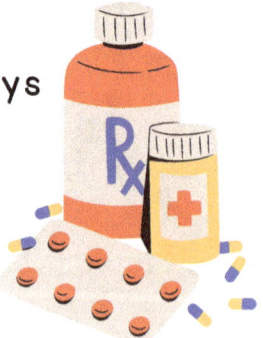

9. Spell:
_____ is going to the shopping mall on Saturday?

Spelling 1-11

10. Spell:

The Headteacher told _____

Brown about the outing.

11. Spell:

_____. Smith is

the new cook.

12. Spell:

_____ without

Jack, the team won the game.

You have finished the words in lesson 11. Fantastic! Don't give up! Keep your eyes ahead to the next lesson.

spelling 1-12

1. Spell:

Barbie used to be my favorite

_____ when I was

a little girl.

2. Spell:

I like to push my toy _____ .

3. Spell:

Swallows usually return to the same site

to make their _____ each

Spring.

Spelling 1-12

4. Spell:

I have a _____ of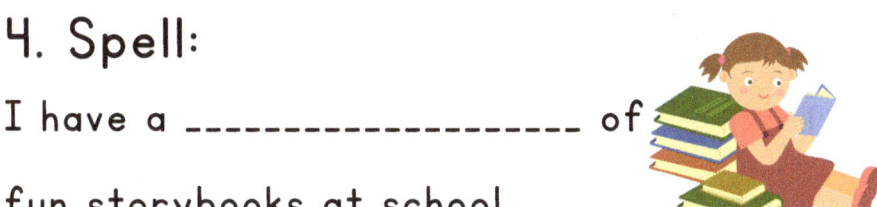

fun storybooks at school.

5. Spell:

The view of the full _____

by the seaside is spectacular.

6. Spell:

We _____ want toys

for our Christmas presents.

Spelling 1-12

7. Spell:

Driving a _____ without a driving license is dangerous and against the law.

8. Spell:

Abigail wore a _____ jacket to school.

9. Spell:

My brother spilled his tea on the _____.

Spelling 1-12

10. Spell:

He arrived in the town by plane and

_____ took a taxi

home.

11. Spell:

_____ house has a big

garden.

12. Spell:

I am an only _____ .

> You have done a great job finishing words in lesson 12. With this rhythm, you are about to be a master in spelling soon.

Spelling 1-13

1. Spell:

My _____ has three bedrooms.

2. Spell:

We should knock on the _____ before we enter a room.

3. Spell:

My mother always gives a penny to the _____ man outside the church.

Spelling 1-13

4. Spell:
Did you _____ your car keys?

5. Spell:
Please, _____ your business and do not talk about my personal life.

6. Spell:
The _____ is wet.

Spelling 1-13

7. Spell:

I am going home _____ I am tired.

8. Spell:

Julia is always _____ to me.

9. Spell:

I am standing _____ the tree.

Spelling 1-13

10. Spell:
I have not seen a bigger boat in my _____ life.

11. Spell:
She _____ off the chair.

12. Spell:
Tim _____ hay fever and should go to the doctor.

Congrats! You have made such Progress! You finished the words in lesson 13 already. Don't forget to practice new vocabulary every week. First, learn the meaning of the word and the spelling of it. Then surprise everyone with your spelling skills.

Spelling 1-14

1. Spell:

I _____ you I would do my homework when I finished eating.

2. Spell:

_____ girl in my class is intelligent.

3. Spell:

_____ news! John passed the exam!

spelling 1-14

4. Spell:

I made a promise, and I will not

_____ it.

5. Spell:

I like eating _____

with my fries.

6. Spell:

My mum is always _____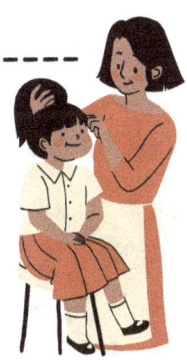

with her work.

Spelling 1-14

7. Spell:

Many _____ are coming to watch the match.

8. Spell:

Sandra is a _____ girl.

9. Spell:

Helen is a _____ girl.

Spelling 1-14

10. Spell:
I will come to your house _____ school today.

11. Spell:
I am very _____ at running 100 metres sprints.

12. Spell:
My team came _____ in the game.

What progress! You completed lesson 14 already. You should be proud of yourself!

Spelling 1-15

1. Spell:
You should better leave the _____ behind and go on with your life.

2. Spell:
My_____ is a police officer.

3. Spell:
My_____ is fun because of my fantastic teacher.

Spelling 1-15

4. Spell:

Planet earth consists of 75%

_____ .

5. Spell:

Kate, please do not be so late to return

to the house _____

6. Spell:

The _____ is green.

Spelling 1-15

7. Spell:

If you _____ the

exams, I will buy you a tablet.

8. Spell:

You must water the _____

for it to grow.

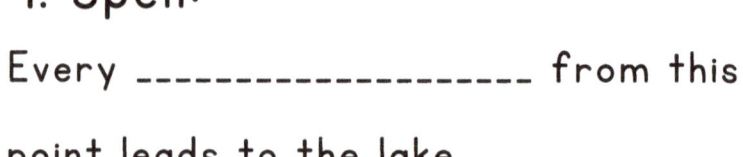

9. Spell:

Every _____ from this

point leads to the lake.

Spelling 1-15

10. Spell:
Elizabeth had a _____

in the morning.

11. Spell:
The bus takes an _____

to arrive at school.

12. Spell:
My teacher will _____

Ella from my class next term.

Wonderful! You have completed words in lesson 15. Keep up the excellent work, and don't forget: Words matter, and most importantly, correctly written words matter.

Spelling 1-16

1. Spell:

This silk shirt is so _____.

2. Spell:

I walked _____ the road to meet my dad.

3. Spell:

My sister can _____ a house.

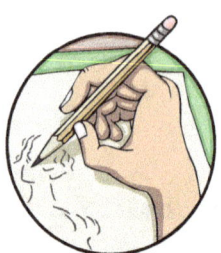

Spelling 1-16

4. Spell:

There is no _____

here for more toys.

5. Spell:

Jude plays the _____

at church.

6. Spell:

Ethan sits at the _____

of the class.

Spelling 1-16

7. Spell:

The _____ hopped over my grandmother's foot.

8. Spell:

_____, sweet _____, said mom after returning from vacation.

9. Spell:

Mrs. Jones took _____ for a swimming lesson.

Spelling 1-16

10. Spell:
She is so talented at singing that she could become a shining _____.

11. Spell:
Oh _____! I think I lost my wallet!

12. Spell:
I am _____ going the football match today.

You're almost finished with becoming a spelling master. You are doing so well! You have completed words in spelling lesson 16. Bravo!

Spelling 1-17

1. Spell:

Ella _____ long black hair.

2. Spell:

I will come to your house _____ you invite me.

3. Spell:

My dad put the fish in the _____.

Spelling 1-17

4. Spell:

The _____ are

coming to repair my house.

5. Spell:

The _____ apple

was thrown away.

6. Spell:

Bella will _____

me up after school.

Spelling 1-17

7. Spell:

We ate hotdogs after the movie was _____.

8. Spell:

How _____ your trip to the Bahamas?

9. Spell:

Every Christmas, I _____ Christmas card to my grandparents.

Spelling 1-17

10. Spell:

The black _____ is under my bed.

11. Spell:

I learned to _____ in the pool.

12. Spell:

_____ is my best friend.

Fantastic! You have completed lesson 17! You're almost done. Don't quit now! You are close to the end.

spelling 1-18

1. Spell:

My _____ is coming to my party.

2. Spell:

I like my _____.

3. Spell:

I was _____ a toddler.

Spelling 1-18

4. Spell:

_____on, mom! Why can't I play a little more with the tablet?

5. Spell:

_____ of my books are in the bookcase.

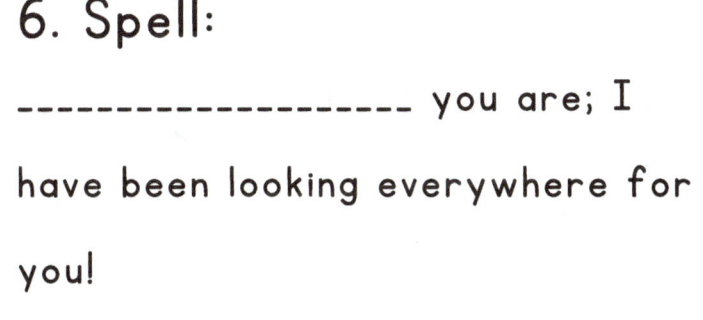

6. Spell:

_____ you are; I have been looking everywhere for you!

Spelling 1-18

7. Spell:

_____ are seven days in a week.

8. Spell:

_____ are you going on Saturday?

9. Spell:
I _____ dancing.

Spelling 1-18

10. Spell:

I can _____ the trolley.

11. Spell:

I can _____ the rope.

12. Spell:

My cup is _____ of water.

Spelling lesson 18 is over! You finished it and, more importantly, learned the lesson's words. However, if you have doubts about one or more words, do not worry; return to it and make as many revisions as necessary.

Spelling 1-19

I. Spell:

The _____ is on

the sea.

2. Spell:

John proposed to Mary with a

diamond _____ .

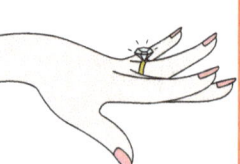

3. Spell:

Ok, Mark, I'll _____ you

tonight at the cinema.

Spelling 1-19

4. Spell:

I got a new _____

for my birthday.

5. Spell:

_____ is six years

older than his sister.

6. Spell:

She does the same as

_____.

Spelling 1-19

7. Spell:

The chips were _____

and crispy.

8. Spell:

Let's _____ this

exercise and go to the next

one.

9. Spell:

I am going to my _____

lesson on Friday.

Spelling 1-19

10. Spell:

My favourite _____ lasagne.

11. Spell:

_____ you seen my

glasses?

12. Spell:

Helen was a _____ friend to

my little brother when he

was sad.

Excellent work, kid! You have made it! You are so close to the end. Lesson 19 is complete. One more task is left, and you are done with Spelling one. Right? Okay, let's go!

Spelling 1-20

1. Spell:
Dorothy has a _____ dolly.

2. Spell:
Emily will _____ at it later today.

3. Spell:
Children should not take their heads out of the car _____ .

Spelling 1-20

4. Spell:
I will take the test on the last

_____ of school.

5. Spell:
The country's young _____

joined the army and went to war.

6. Spell:
I had a restful _____

yesterday.

Spelling 1-20

7. Spell:

I met a nice _____ at the bus stop today.

8. Spell:

Joshua's brother will _____ if you take the remote away.

9. Spell:

_____ the rain, the soil was wet.

spelling 1-20

10. Spell:

Going to _____ makes you learn new things and meet new friends.

11. Spell:

The radio plays my favorite _____.

12. Spell:

My _____ are traveling to New York next week.

Congrats! You have finished learning the words in spelling one.

Conclusion

Congratulations, you little spelling heroes!

You have arrived at the end of Spelling 1! You have made it, and you should be proud of yourself! Now you can give yourself a round of applause for getting this far.

I hope that finishing Spelling 1 has boosted your confidence in your vocabulary knowledge and your spelling skills with 240 words.

However, if you got some words incorrect, no worries; we all learn at different paces and in our own time. No judgement here. To improve your "weak spots", you can always return to and revise the words you found the hardest to grasp and have another look at their spelling or try to remember their meaning.

And don't forget that repeating the words you got wrong about 5 times can bring you back to the masters level and prepare you for the next challenge!

So, that's it folks!
See you in Spelling 2

Spelling Two

An Interactive Vocabulary & Spelling Workbook for 6 Year Olds.

Introduction

Are you ready to get to the next milestone?

Spelling two is the second Spelling for Kids series book and will cover 264 words.

It is ideal for six-year-olds. It's up to you to hear them, understand them, learn their spelling, and finally, learn to write them down correctly.

If you follow the instructions I have already given you, it will be a piece of cake! Remember first to hear the word, then read it in the sentence, write it down, and check its spelling.

You can do it as often as possible to ensure you fully grasp each word and remember its spelling.

Practice makes perfect, after all.

So...on your marks, get set, go!

Spelling 2-1

1. Spell:

Lexie will _____ you some

of her crayons for your coloring.

2. Spell:

Tyler_____ his drink

to his sister.

3. Spell:

_____ still so that we can

take a photo.

Spelling 2-1

4. Spell:

_____ this dress suit me?

5. Spell:

Beth has a _____

bag.

6. Spell:

The school bus had already

_____

before we finished breakfast.

Spelling 2-1

7. Spell:
Kitty got a _____ ticket for the show.

8. Spell:
Rose has a pink _____ for her birthday.

9. Spell:
The entrance _____ is open.

Spelling 2-1

10. Spell:

Callum had a cup of _____ with biscuits.

11. Spell:

_____ Tom, it's been a long time since your last visit, and I want to know if you are well.

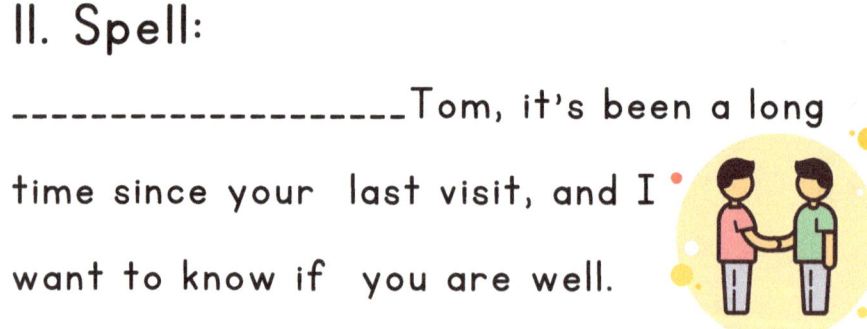

12. Spell:

I can not _____ my pencil.

That's it for lesson 1... So you can enjoy the rest of your fantastic day!

Spelling 2-2

1. Spell:
I _____ my mum driving off the driveway.

2. Spell:
I am _____ that I got all my sums right.

3. Spell:
I tried my _____ in the timetabling challenge today.

Spelling 2-2

4. Spell:

_____ of my friend is going to the hospital today.

5. Spell:

Lucy and Emma are _____ their homework together.

6. Spell:

I will be _____ swimming on Saturday.

spelling 2-2

7. Spell:
There are seven days in a

_____.

Sun
Mon
Tue
Wed
Thu
Fri
Sat

8. Spell:
I gave the dog a _____ to chew.

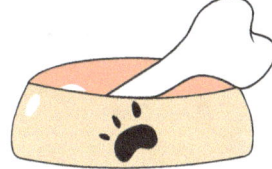

9. Spell:
My birthday party will _____ a lot of money.

Spelling 2-2

10. Spell:
The rocket disappeared in the _____ soon after taking off.

11. Spell:
My family is going _____ on holiday to Dubai.

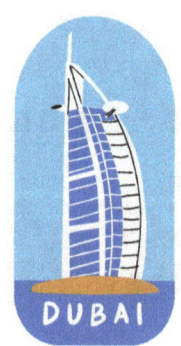

12. Spell:
Dylan _____ seven years old.

Congrats! You have finished learning the words in lesson 2. Remember to know and understand the meaning of all the new words you have found.

Spelling 2-3

1. Spell:

There are _____ questions in the spelling test.

2. Spell:

I got 12 questions out _____ the 12 questions in the assessment.

3. Spell:

I _____ a lot of vegetables with my rice.

and

Spelling 2-3

4. Spell:
My mother tells me a _____ before I fall asleep.

5. Spell:
The Headteacher gave us a _____ time to play because we were naughty.

6. Spell:
I like bacon _____ my eggs.

Spelling 2-3

7. Spell:
Jude will _____ you some money for your transport.

8. Spell:
We bought a _____ of bread for our breakfast.

9. Spell:
The School choir will sing _____ the hall.

Spelling 2-3

10. Spell:
The best _____ to do is apologize to him.

11. Spell:
I have never _____ anyone his secret.

12. Spell:
I _____ my brother to come to my school.

> You've made it! You completed lesson 3. Pay attention, kids; if you find it difficult to learn some words, you should write them down on paper. That will help you remember them better.

spelling 2-4

1. Spell:
Tommy will _____ his football lessons on Sunday.

2. Spell:
Are _____ the drawings you made at school?

3. Spell:
_____ swimming in the sea, we built castles in the sand.

spelling 2-4

4. Spell:

Anthony walked _____

the road to get some drinks.

5. Spell:

I am making a jam sandwich for

_____ .

6. Spell:

The children _____ sitting

quietly in the room.

Spelling 2-4

7. Spell:

Amelia will be _____ to my house on Sunday.

8. Spell:

The _____ is green.

9. Spell:

We will _____ the classroom tidy.

Spelling 2-4

10. Spell:

She said the same thing _____.

11. Spell:

Come on and _____ my day,

Tim! Tell me some good news.

12. Spell:

Daniel did _____ the

ball into the road.

Great! Lesson 4 is over! I suggest you get some rest before going on to the next lesson. That will help you recharge and return to the next task more refreshed! Great work!

Spelling 2-5

1. Spell:
You can _____ your eyes now and search for the hideout.

2. Spell:
There are many pencils _____ my pencil case.

3. Spell:
I _____ a tuna sandwich with my mum.

spelling 2-5

4. Spell:

Jesse has only one _____.

5. Spell:

Aaron had an _____ sandwich

for two days in a row.

6. Spell:

What are we having for

_____, mom?

Spelling 2-5

7. Spell:

The cheetah can run _____.

8. Spell:

My dad works every day from nine to

_____.

9. Spell:

Joe _____ second in

the long jump.

Spelling 2-5

10. Spell:

Tracy put an _____

pack on her swollen finger.

11. Spell:

My sister is three years _____.

12. Spell:

The new-born did _____

for her mum.

Fantastic! You have finished the words in lesson 5. What a task! Kids, keep a note: An easy way to learn the majority of new words is to break them apart; in that way, the words can be easily organized from the shortest to the longest.

Spelling 2-6

1. Spell:
Ella was the _____

girl to win the contest ever.

WIN

2. Spell:
The _____ whistled when it

arrived at the station.

3. Spell:
_____ is taking Alfie

to his guitar lesson?

Spelling 2-6

4. Spell:

Never cross the _____ before looking first from both sides.

5. Spell:

_____ is necessary for life on the planet.

6. Spell:

Karen is an old _____ of my brother.

Spelling 2-6

7. Spell:
Wearing a seat belt keeps you _____ in case of a car accident.

8. Spell:
After the earthquake, we slept in a _____ for one week.

9. Spell:
Abigail did _____ a boat in the race.

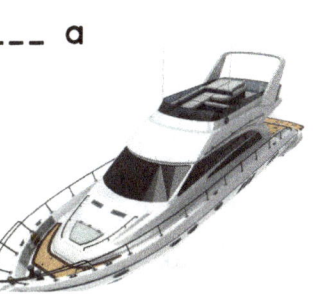

Spelling 2-6

10. Spell:

It will be _____ if you can come to my brother's wedding.

11. Spell:

Daniel put the bird in the white _____ .

12. Spell:

Oliver has a round _____ with freckles.

Lesson 6 has come to an end. Awesome! Keep up the excellent work! And do not forget: Repetition makes the master!

Spelling 2-7

1. Spell:
The teenager helped the old lady

_____

her shopping trolley.

2. Spell:
She played a _____ on him.

3. Spell:
_____ you coming along with me?

Spelling 2-7

4. Spell:

Ben was not _____ his work in class, so I told the teacher.

5. Spell:

_____ of my friends are going to the dance tomorrow.

6. Spell:

We have a new _____ in our kitchen.

Spelling 2-7

7. Spell:

The _____ says seven o'clock.

8. Spell:

I can _____ the road on my own.

9. Spell:

I have _____ brothers.

Spelling 2-7

10. Spell:

I had an _____ with my breakfast.

11. Spell:

Jude enjoyed having the _____ mango.

12. Spell:

With _____ and butter, you can make your breakfast.

Look at how far you have gone! You have reached and completed lesson 7! What a student you are! Congratulations!

Spelling 2-8

1. Spell:
Ella will _____ my hair when she comes.

2. Spell:
The _____ is full of water.

3. Spell:
We had a fun lesson with Mrs. Smith in _____ today.

Spelling 2-8

4. Spell:
Elizabeth goes to _____ with her family every Sunday.

5. Spell:
Julius was _____ when he heard that his parents were breaking up.

6. Spell:
They interrupted the program to report a breaking _____.

Spelling 2-8

7. Spell:
Molly walks about a _____

to school every day.

8. Spell:
Billy pushed the shopping _____

for his grandmother.

9. Spell:
The _____ loaded the

cart with tomatoes.

Spelling 2-8

10. Spell:

The back _____ has lovely flowers.

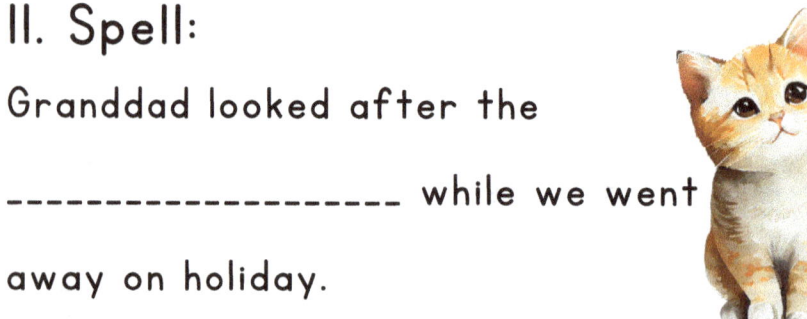

11. Spell:

Granddad looked after the _____ while we went away on holiday.

12. Spell:

Dark clouds always bring _____ .

> Look at you! You are natural! And it seems that you will be a spelling bee master pretty soon! You have just finished lesson 8.

Spelling 2-9

1. Spell:
A _____ has four legs.

2. Spell:
The _____ girl was timid.

3. Spell:
I will _____ my mum if you can come for a sleepover today.

Spelling 2-9

4. Spell:
After the sunset, the stars appeared in the _____ .

5. Spell:
Lily threatened to _____ the wood house down.

6. Spell:
I like my mummy _____ daddy.

Spelling 2-9

7. Spell:
Buying a _____ coat can be very expensive.

8. Spell:
Megan got a new _____ pencil case.

9. Spell:
Sheila will _____ the water in her water bottle.

Spelling 2-9

10. Spell:
Tina was _____ to the old lady by standing up for her on the bus.

11. Spell:
He left the front door open, and the cat was _____ .

12. Spell:
I bought this doll during the sale at _____ price.

Well done! You have finished lesson 9. You should be proud of yourself! And remember this: Always enunciate each word properly; this method will help you spell the word correctly.

Spelling 2-10

1. Spell:

Keep your _____ up

to look more confident.

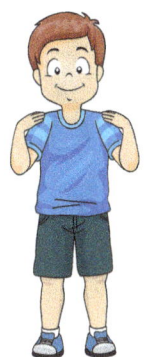

2. Spell:

Tom poured his drink into a

_____ cup.

3. Spell:

Teddy polished his pair of

_____ with his grandad.

Spelling 2-10

4. Spell:
The test will _____

after an hour.

5. Spell:
You should _____ saving

money to buy a car.

6. Spell:
Bella found it hard to stir the

_____ soup.

Spelling 2-10

7. Spell:

Lucy has bought her train

_____ for the trip.

8. Spell:

Come on, _____!

Get on that dance floor!

9. Spell:

My dad has enough _____ to

pay for a new car.

Spelling 2-10

10. Spell:
Doing spelling exercises helps you _____ your spelling skills.

11. Spell:
The _____ shook hands with everyone in the match.

12. Spell:
If you want a _____ lunch, buy a sandwich.

> You completed lesson 10! Bravo! You are doing a great job. Pretty soon, you will be an expert in spelling.

Spelling 2-11

1. Spell:
The Headteacher will be spending the

_____ term in

a new school.

2. Spell:
Bob wears two jumpers during the

_____ months.

3. Spell:
Bob did not have _____

money on him.

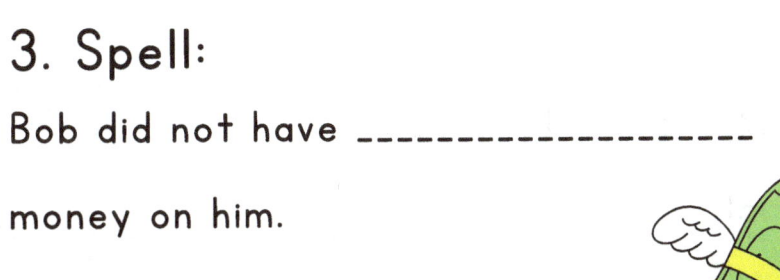

Spelling 2-11

4. Spell:

Ben is not good at _____

animals, but he paints them well.

5. Spell:

How _____ rulers

are in your pencil case?

6. Spell:

The little girl did _____ under

the table.

Spelling 2-11

7. Spell:

Sue wore a _____

dress for the choir rehearsal.

8. Spell:

Bill is going _____

next week to New York.

9. Spell:

Ted is now _____

confident in his two-times table

after much practice.

Spelling 2-11

10. Spell:

Anthony is wearing a red cap on his

_____ .

11. Spell:

Jude was able to _____ the secret box.

12. Spell:

I will _____ my parents my report card after school.

Great work! You have completed lesson 11.

Spelling 2-12

1. Spell:
Mr. Oliver had to _____ because all the seats were taken on the train.

2. Spell:
Jane can _____ her dog.

3. Spell:
She came to the shop _____ midday.

Spelling 2-12

4. Spell:

I _____ I should do my spelling right away.

5. Spell:

I did _____ in my spelling at school after practicing at home with my spelling book.

6. Spell:

He fell _____ as soon as his face touched the pillow.

Spelling 2-12

7. Spell:
We _____ the hidden treasure with the help of this old map.

8. Spell:
The teacher asked the class to _____ up the mess on the floor.

9. Spell:
The bus for the excursion was _____ of people.

Spelling 2-12

10. Spell:

There are lots of red cars on the

_____.

11. Spell:

Mr. Philip told the class an exciting

_____ .

12. Spell:

The school dinner is going to be yummy on

_____.

You have done a great job finishing words in lesson 12. With this rhythm, you are about to be a master in spelling soon.

Spelling 2-13

1. Spell:
Every Sunday we go for a picnic at the

_____ .

2. Spell:
Tonight's _____ is a

popular TV series.

3. Spell:
Loretta loves her _____

dolly.

Spelling 2-13

4. Spell:

Jane helped her mum _____

the dishes.

5. Spell:

The school uniform is a grey

_____ and a white

blouse.

6. Spell:

I brush my teeth every _____

after having breakfast.

Spelling 2-13

7. Spell:
A massive _____ of smoke came from the factory.

8. Spell:
Billy knows how to _____ a horse and will participate in the horsing games.

9. Spell:
Logan's _____ stood still for Tom to brush his hair.

Spelling 2-13

10. Spell:
Mr. Fisher does not trust

_____ in the class.

11. Spell:
That was the worst score that I have

_____ had on any test.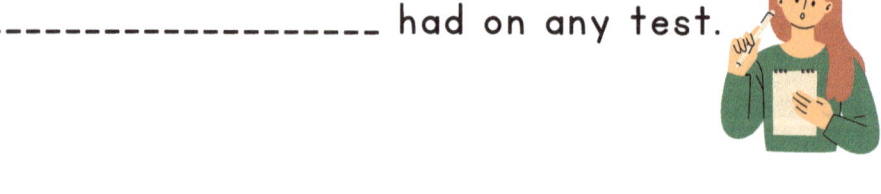

12. Spell:
I will _____ be rude

to my teachers.

Congrats! You have made such Progress! You finished the words in lesson 13 already. Don't forget to practice new vocabulary every week. First, learn the meaning of the word and the spelling of it. Then surprise everyone with your spelling skills.

Spelling 2-14

1. Spell:
The cat kept _____ at the lady.

2. Spell:
The toy store is right after the _____ of the road.

3. Spell:
The _____ alarm in the room is not working.

Spelling 2-14

4. Spell:
You need _____ to make a cake.

5. Spell:
We are going to _____ some money at the beach on ice lollies.

6. Spell:
Fishes live in the _____ .

Spelling 2-14

7. Spell:

_____ are twenty children in our class.

8. Spell:

Benny could not keep _____ after 9 pm.

9. Spell:

_____ was Nathan's christening.

Spelling 2-14

10. Spell:

_____ is your name?

11. Spell:

Where is _____

spelling book?

12. Spell:

Ella is going to her dance lesson

on _____ .

What progress! You completed lesson 14 already. You should be proud of yourself!

Spelling 2-15

1. Spell:
Billy can drive a big _____ .

2. Spell:
The _____ clothes are

in the washing machine.

3. Spell:
The lesson ends at

_____ o'clock.

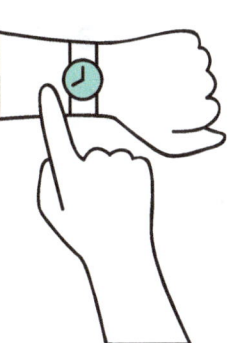

Spelling 2-15

4. Spell:

I am Sam; what's your _____?

5. Spell:

_____ is Monday.

6. Spell:

The baby will not _____ if you take his toy away.

Spelling 2-15

7. Spell:

She took a _____ with her Nanny.

8. Spell:

The dog is _____ old, and he cannot hear well.

9. Spell:

Denis heard _____ talking in the next room.

Spelling 2-15

10. Spell:

What is _____ name?

11. Spell:

_____ is bothering me in this situation, but I can not tell what exactly.

12. Spell:

Alfie is going for his football training on _____ .

Wonderful! You have completed words in lesson 15. Keep up the excellent work, and don't forget: Words matter, and most importantly, correctly written words matter.

Spelling 2-16

1. Spell:

Joseph crossed the _____

with his mummy.

2. Spell:

Hey Mark, come _____

with me to play football.

3. Spell:

The soldiers _____ up

in rows for the military parade.

Spelling 2-16

4. Spell:

_____ names are on the class register.

5. Spell:

The old lady called _____ for help.

6. Spell:

Jude and James are going to a _____ party on Saturday.

Spelling 2-16

7. Spell:

Jesus _____ on

the cross for all our sins.

8. Spell:

There are twelve months in a

_____ .

9. Spell:

My mom wears earplugs when she sleeps

because she doesn't want to

_____ dad snoring.

Spelling 2-16

10. Spell:

Always _____ your

bike with your helmet on.

11. Spell:

Jake did not _____ his

sentence with a full stop.

12. Spell:

The carpenter came to _____

the broken table.

You have done a great job finishing words in lesson 16. With this rhythm, you are about to be a master in spelling soon.

Spelling 2-17

1. Spell:

Can you spell your _____,

please?

2. Spell:

What do you want to use the pencil

_____ ?

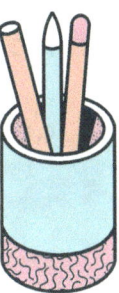

3. Spell:

I will keep my promise, and I will

never _____ you.

Spelling 2-17

4. Spell:

The Snow Queen wore a

_____ gown.

5. Spell:

The cowboy threw a _____

to catch the cow.

6. Spell:

Julia could not go out _____

it was raining.

Spelling 2-17

7. Spell:

The chair is _____ the table.

8. Spell:

My gran grew the _____ flower in her garden.

9. Spell:

The _____ conditioner is on, so we have a low temperature in the house.

spelling 2-17

10. Spell:

She opened the _____ to get some fresh air into the room.

11. Spell:

My older brother worked as a lifeguard last _____ .

12. Spell:

You always fight like a cat and _____ .

Fantastic! You have completed spelling lesson 17! You're almost done.

Spelling 2-18

1. Spell:
Jude forgot to mail his _____ the letter.

2. Spell:
The boys have _____ to school.

3. Spell:
Daniel is _____ to the match on Saturday.

Spelling 2-18

4. Spell:

David spoke clearly and confidently in

_____ of the

whole class.

5. Spell:

It's _____ outside; it seems

that it is going to snow.

6. Spell:

_____ is the time to keep

quiet.

Spelling 2-18

7. Spell:

I will never _____ my dad's advice.

8. Spell:

Who is _____ for vaccination?

9. Spell:

_____ Balance is a popular sneakers trademark.

Spelling 2-18

10. Spell:

The swimming instructor will

_____ him out of the pool.

11. Spell:

_____ tea is served at 5:00pm.

12. Spell:

Seize the _____ and make the

best of it.

You are doing so well! You have completed words in spelling lesson 18. Bravo!

Spelling 2-19

1. Spell:
Elizabeth got a new piano for her

_____ presents.

2. Spell:

_____ before you speak.

3. Spell:
There is a _____ fountain in

the school playground.

Spelling 2-19

4. Spell:
My _____ plays football and Rugby.

5. Spell:
Five is more _____ two.

6. Spell:
I walk to school on _____ .

Spelling 2-19

7. Spell:

He offered me his _____

to sit because I felt dizzy.

8. Spell:

I drew a rose _____ for

my mum on mother's day.

9. Spell:

We are having _____

with our grandmother on

Saturday.

Spelling 2-19

10. Spell:
The house where I grew up is _____ of my childhood memories.

11. Spell:
All the girls wore _____ uniforms to school.

12. Spell:
_____ is the sheep's hair, and it keeps them very warm.

You have finished the words in lesson 19. Fantastic!

Spelling 2-20

1. Spell:

_____ your life to the fullest!

2. Spell:

It will _____ you lesser money if you buy it on sales.

3. Spell:

Billy rode his _____ on Sunday.

Spelling 2-20

4. Spell:
Billy _____ his wallet at the playground.

5. Spell:
I like to _____ up the balloons when the party is over.

6. Spell:
I will start to draw the cat on a new _____ .

Spelling 2-20

7. Spell:

Steven won the _____ medal.

8. Spell:

Ella wrote a _____ to her penfriend in Germany.

9. Spell:

Luke was _____ in confronting the bully in his class.

Spelling 2-20

10. Spell:

_____ you pass me the salt, please?

11. Spell:

Kitty _____ be practicing her spelling instead of singing.

12. Spell:

The baby _____ cry if you tease him.

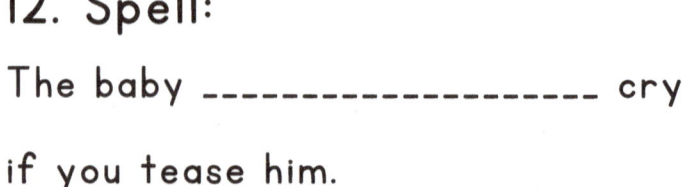

Spelling lesson 20 is over. You finished it and, more importantly, learned the lesson's words. However, if you have doubts about one or more words, do not worry; return to the word and make as many revisions as necessary.

Spelling 2-21

1. Spell:

Ben wore a white _____ for the occasion.

2. Spell:

My mum bought me _____ pair of trainers.

3. Spell:

_____ night is pizza night for this family.

Spelling 2-21

4. Spell:
We _____ all be taking part in the drama.

5. Spell:
My uncle and his wife had a good view of the _____ .

6. Spell:
I will be in a new _____ in September.

Spelling 2-21

7. Spell:

The teacher advised my sister to read

_____ books.

8. Spell:

The teacher allowed the students to have

a _____ break.

9. Spell:

The older man left the

_____ last week.

Spelling 2-21

10. Spell:
I can hear you very well, and you don't have to _____ !

11. Spell:
In _____ , the flowers blossom.

12. Spell:
We learned how to write an informative _____ today at school.

Excellent work, kid! You have made it! You are so close to the end. Lesson 21 is complete. One more task is left, and you are done with spelling 2. Right? Okay, let's go!

Spelling 2-22

1. Spell:
Sanjay bought a new pair of
_____ trainers.

2. Spell:
Let's play _____ and
seek.

3. Spell:
The ball is _____
the table.

Spelling 2-22

4. Spell:
The pencil is _____ .

5. Spell:
The _____ was locked, but the thief managed to break the lock and get into the house.

6. Spell:
Magdalene is a _____ friend.

Spelling 2-22

7. Spell:
Ted dropped the letter in the

_____ .

8. Spell:
Jude will go to his swimming lessons

on _____ .

9. Spell:
_____ student must

have a student card.

Spelling 2-22

10. Spell:

Did you _____ the noise that came from the garden?

11. Spell:

The class teacher gave us a _____ each for being sensible in the school choir.

12. Spell:

Mary looks good in _____ colors.

Congrats! You have finished learning the words in spelling 2.

Please leave a 1-click Review!

I would be incredibly thankful if you could take just 60 seconds to write a brief review on Amazon or the platform of purchase, even if it's just a few sentences!

Conclusion

CONGRATULATIONS, you little spelling champions!

You have finally finished Spelling 2!

Well done! Do you hear the trumpets sound?

Well, I do! And you should take pride in yourself. And the same goes for your guardians, parents, or teacher!

By now, you should be capable of spelling 264 more new words. Two hundred and sixty-four new words are added to your vocabulary. Boy, isn't that a small triumph?

I bet you already feel more confident in your spelling skills. However, don't get too much confidence though. Remember to make the necessary revisions to ensure you know the words' dictation and meaning. And if by any chance some words seem to bother you, focus on them by repeating the practice. Repetition makes the master; don't you ever forget that.

Our next appointment is with Spelling 3.
See you there!

Answers

Spelling 1-1

1. Spell: <u>A</u>
2. Spell: <u>Do</u>
3. Spell: <u>To</u>
4. Spell: <u>Of</u>
5. Spell: <u>Says</u>
6. Spell: <u>Be</u>
7. Spell: <u>Me</u>
8. Spell: <u>One</u>
9. Spell: <u>Any</u>
10. Spell: <u>Go</u>
11. Spell: <u>So</u>
12. Spell: <u>By</u>

Spelling 1-2

1. Spell: <u>And</u>
2. Spell: <u>Big</u>
3. Spell: <u>Ant</u>
4. Spell: <u>Hot</u>
5. Spell: <u>By</u>
6. Spell: <u>Put</u>
7. Spell: <u>Run</u>
8. Spell: <u>On</u>
9. Spell: <u>Did</u>
10. Spell: <u>Boy</u>
11. Spell: <u>From</u>
12. Spell: <u>Cot</u>

Answers

Spelling 1-3

1. Spell: <u>Are</u>
2. Spell: <u>Saw</u>
3. Spell: <u>You</u>
4. Spell: <u>Yes</u>
5. Spell: <u>Bus</u>
6. Spell: <u>The</u>
7. Spell: <u>Ran</u>
8. Spell: <u>Sit</u>
9. Spell: <u>Nuts</u>
10. Spell: <u>Cup</u>
11. Spell: <u>Her</u>
12. Spell: <u>Job</u>

Spelling 1-4

1. Spell: <u>Flag</u>
2. Spell: <u>He</u>
3. Spell: <u>We</u>
4. Spell: <u>Leg</u>
5. Spell: <u>Cow</u>
6. Spell: <u>Fun</u>
7. Spell: <u>Big</u>
8. Spell: <u>No</u>
9. Spell: <u>Him</u>
10. Spell: <u>His</u>
11. Spell: <u>Us</u>
12. Spell: <u>She</u>

Answers

Spelling 1-5

1. Spell: <u>Dad</u>
2. Spell: <u>Book</u>
3. Spell: <u>Tree</u>
4. Spell: <u>Run</u>
5. Spell: <u>Went</u>
6. Spell: <u>Yes</u>
7. Spell: <u>With</u>
8. Spell: <u>My</u>
9. Spell: <u>Dog</u>
10. Spell: <u>For</u>
11. Spell: <u>Leg</u>
12. Spell: <u>Man</u>

Spelling 1-6

1. Spell: <u>My</u>
2. Spell: <u>Ask</u>
3. Spell: <u>Put</u>
4. Spell: <u>Was</u>
5. Spell: <u>Is</u>
6. Spell: <u>Has</u>
7. Spell: <u>You</u>
8. Spell: <u>Said</u>
9. Spell: <u>Your</u>
10. Spell: <u>They</u>
11. Spell: <u>Were</u>
12. Spell: <u>Today</u>

Answers

Spelling 1-7

1. Spell: <u>Win</u>
2. Spell: <u>Has</u>
3. Spell: <u>Girl</u>
4. Spell: <u>I</u>
5. Spell: <u>Good</u>
6. Spell: <u>Help</u>
7. Spell: <u>Six</u>
8. Spell: <u>Tap</u>
9. Spell: <u>Do</u>
10. Spell: <u>Sad</u>
11. Spell: <u>Dress</u>
12. Spell: <u>Pet</u>

Spelling 1-8

1. Spell: <u>Mud</u>
2. Spell: <u>Milk</u>
3. Spell: <u>Red</u>
4. Spell: <u>Little</u>
5. Spell: <u>At</u>
6. Spell: <u>The</u>
7. Spell: <u>Get</u>
8. Spell: <u>Jump</u>
9. Spell: <u>Pat</u>
10. Spell: <u>Bird</u>
11. Spell: <u>Baby</u>
12. Spell: <u>Like</u>

Answers

Spelling 1-9

1. Spell: <u>Wild</u>
2. Spell: <u>Most</u>
3. Spell: <u>Both</u>
4. Spell: <u>Children</u>
5. Spell: <u>Climb</u>
6. Spell: <u>Only</u>
7. Spell: <u>Old</u>
8. Spell: <u>Many</u>
9. Spell: <u>Clothes</u>
10. Spell: <u>Cold</u>
11. Spell: <u>Gold</u>
12. Spell: <u>Hold</u>

Spelling 1-10

1. Spell: <u>Past</u>
2. Spell: <u>Father</u>
3. Spell: <u>Class</u>
4. Spell: <u>Water</u>
5. Spell: <u>Again</u>
6. Spell: <u>Grass</u>
7. Spell: <u>Pass</u>
8. Spell: <u>Plant</u>
9. Spell: <u>Path</u>
10. Spell: <u>Bath</u>
11. Spell: <u>Hour</u>
12. Spell: <u>Move</u>

Answers

Spelling 1-11

1. Spell: <u>Prove</u>
2. Spell: <u>Half</u>
3. Spell: <u>Sugar</u>
4. Spell: <u>Could</u>
5. Spell: <u>Would</u>
6. Spell: <u>Sure</u>
7. Spell: <u>Eve</u>
8. Spell: <u>Should</u>
9. Spell: <u>Who</u>
10. Spell: <u>Mr</u>
11. Spell: <u>Mrs</u>
12. Spell: <u>Even</u>

Spelling 1-12

1. Spell: <u>Doll</u>
2. Spell: <u>Pram</u>
3. Spell: <u>Nest</u>
4. Spell: <u>Lot</u>
5. Spell: <u>Moon</u>
6. Spell: <u>All</u>
7. Spell: <u>Car</u>
8. Spell: <u>Red</u>
9. Spell: <u>Rug</u>
10. Spell: <u>Then</u>
11. Spell: <u>Our</u>
12. Spell: <u>Child</u>

Answers

Spelling 1-13

1. Spell: <u>Prove</u>
2. Spell: <u>Half</u>
3. Spell: <u>Sugar</u>
4. Spell: <u>Could</u>
5. Spell: <u>Would</u>
6. Spell: <u>Sure</u>
7. Spell: <u>Eve</u>
8. Spell: <u>Should</u>
9. Spell: <u>Who</u>
10. Spell: <u>Mr</u>
11. Spell: <u>Mrs</u>
12. Spell: <u>Even</u>

Spelling 1-14

1. Spell: <u>Told</u>
2. Spell: <u>Every</u>
3. Spell: <u>Great</u>
4. Spell: <u>Break</u>
5. Spell: <u>Steak</u>
6. Spell: <u>Busy</u>
7. Spell: <u>People</u>
8. Spell: <u>Pretty</u>
9. Spell: <u>Beautiful</u>
10. Spell: <u>After</u>
11. Spell: <u>Fast</u>
12. Spell: <u>Last</u>

Answers

Spelling 1-15

1. Spell: <u>Past</u>
2. Spell: <u>Father</u>
3. Spell: <u>Class</u>
4. Spell: <u>Water</u>
5. Spell: <u>Again</u>
6. Spell: <u>Grass</u>
7. Spell: <u>Pass</u>
8. Spell: <u>Plant</u>
9. Spell: <u>Path</u>
10. Spell: <u>Bath</u>
11. Spell: <u>Hour</u>
12. Spell: <u>Move</u>

Spelling 1-16

1. Spell: <u>Soft</u>
2. Spell: <u>Down</u>
3. Spell: <u>Draw</u>
4. Spell: <u>Room</u>
5. Spell: <u>Drum</u>
6. Spell: <u>Back</u>
7. Spell: <u>Frog</u>
8. Spell: <u>Home</u>
9. Spell: <u>Them</u>
10. Spell: <u>Star</u>
11. Spell: <u>Boy</u>
12. Spell: <u>Not</u>

Answers

Spelling 1-17

1. Spell: <u>Has</u>
2. Spell: <u>If</u>
3. Spell: <u>Pond</u>
4. Spell: <u>Men</u>
5. Spell: <u>Bad</u>
6. Spell: <u>Pick</u>
7. Spell: <u>Over</u>
8. Spell: <u>Was</u>
9. Spell: <u>Send</u>
10. Spell: <u>Box</u>
11. Spell: <u>Swim</u>
12. Spell: <u>She</u>

Spelling 1-18

1. Spell: <u>Friend</u>
2. Spell: <u>School</u>
3. Spell: <u>Once</u>
4. Spell: <u>Come</u>
5. Spell: <u>Some</u>
6. Spell: <u>Here</u>
7. Spell: <u>There</u>
8. Spell: <u>Where</u>
9. Spell: <u>Love</u>
10. Spell: <u>Push</u>
11. Spell: <u>Pull</u>
12. Spell: <u>Full</u>

Answers

Spelling 1-19

1. Spell: <u>Ship</u>
2. Spell: <u>Ring</u>
3. Spell: <u>See</u>
4. Spell: <u>Dress</u>
5. Spell: <u>He</u>
6. Spell: <u>Me</u>
7. Spell: <u>Thin</u>
8. Spell: <u>Skip</u>
9. Spell: <u>Drum</u>
10. Spell: <u>Food</u>
11. Spell: <u>Have</u>
12. Spell: <u>Good</u>

Spelling 1-20

1. Spell: <u>Pretty</u>
2. Spell: <u>Look</u>
3. Spell: <u>Window</u>
4. Spell: <u>Day</u>
5. Spell: <u>Men</u>
6. Spell: <u>Sleep</u>
7. Spell: <u>Lady</u>
8. Spell: <u>Cry</u>
9. Spell: <u>After</u>
10. Spell: <u>School</u>
11. Spell: <u>Song</u>
12. Spell: <u>Parents</u>

Answers

Spelling 2-1

1. Spell: <u>Give</u>
2. Spell: <u>Gave</u>
3. Spell: <u>Stand</u>
4. Spell: <u>Does</u>
5. Spell: <u>Small</u>
6. Spell: <u>Gone</u>
7. Spell: <u>Free</u>
8. Spell: <u>Cake</u>
9. Spell: <u>Door</u>
10. Spell: <u>Tea</u>
11. Spell: <u>Dear</u>
12. Spell: <u>Find</u>

Spelling 2-2

1. Spell: <u>Saw</u>
2. Spell: <u>Happy</u>
3. Spell: <u>Best</u>
4. Spell: <u>One</u>
5. Spell: <u>Doing</u>
6. Spell: <u>Going</u>
7. Spell: <u>Week</u>
8. Spell: <u>Bone</u>
9. Spell: <u>Cost</u>
10. Spell: <u>Sky</u>
11. Spell: <u>Away</u>
12. Spell: <u>Is</u>

Answers

Spelling 2-3

1. Spell: <u>Nine</u>
2. Spell: <u>Of</u>
3. Spell: <u>Eat</u>
4. Spell: <u>Story</u>
5. Spell: <u>Short</u>
6. Spell: <u>With</u>
7. Spell: <u>Give</u>
8. Spell: <u>Loaf</u>
9. Spell: <u>At</u>
10. Spell: <u>Thing</u>
11. Spell: <u>Told</u>
12. Spell: <u>Want</u>

Spelling 2-4

1. Spell: <u>Stop</u>
2. Spell: <u>These</u>
3. Spell: <u>After</u>
4. Spell: <u>Down</u>
5. Spell: <u>Myself</u>
6. Spell: <u>Were</u>
7. Spell: <u>Coming</u>
8. Spell: <u>Leaf</u>
9. Spell: <u>Keep</u>
10. Spell: <u>Again</u>
11. Spell: <u>Make</u>
12. Spell: <u>Kick</u>

Answers

Spelling 2-5

1. Spell: <u>Open</u>
2. Spell: <u>Inside</u>
3. Spell: <u>Made</u>
4. Spell: <u>Sister</u>
5. Spell: <u>Egg</u>
6. Spell: <u>Dinner</u>
7. Spell: <u>Fast</u>
8. Spell: <u>Five</u>
9. Spell: <u>Came</u>
10. Spell: <u>Ice</u>
11. Spell: <u>Old</u>
12. Spell: <u>Cry</u>

Spelling 2-6

1. Spell: <u>First</u>
2. Spell: <u>Train</u>
3. Spell: <u>Who</u>
4. Spell: <u>Street</u>
5. Spell: <u>Water</u>
6. Spell: <u>Mate</u>
7. Spell: <u>Safe</u>
8. Spell: <u>Tent</u>
9. Spell: <u>Sail</u>
10. Spell: <u>Nice</u>
11. Spell: <u>Cage</u>
12. Spell: <u>Face</u>

Answers

Spelling 2-7

1. Spell: Push
2. Spell: Trick
3. Spell: Are
4. Spell: Doing
5. Spell: Many
6. Spell: Clock
7. Spell: Time
8. Spell: Cross
9. Spell: Two
10. Spell: Apple
11. Spell: Ripe
12. Spell: Bread

Spelling 2-8

1. Spell: Brush
2. Spell: Bucket
3. Spell: Class
4. Spell: Church
5. Spell: Hurt
6. Spell: News
7. Spell: Mile
8. Spell: Cart
9. Spell: Farmer
10. Spell: Garden
11. Spell: Kitten
12. Spell: Rain

Answers

Spelling 2-9

1. Spell: <u>Table</u>
2. Spell: <u>New</u>
3. Spell: <u>Ask</u>
4. Spell: <u>Sky</u>
5. Spell: <u>Burn</u>
6. Spell: <u>And</u>
7. Spell: <u>Fur</u>
8. Spell: <u>Brown</u>
9. Spell: <u>Drink</u>
10. Spell: <u>Kind</u>
11. Spell: <u>Gone</u>
12. Spell: <u>Half</u>

Spelling 2-10

1. Spell: <u>Head</u>
2. Spell: <u>Clean</u>
3. Spell: <u>Shoes</u>
4. Spell: <u>Stop</u>
5. Spell: <u>Begin</u>
6. Spell: <u>Thick</u>
7. Spell: <u>Ticket</u>
8. Spell: <u>Everybody</u>
9. Spell: <u>Money</u>
10. Spell: <u>Improve</u>
11. Spell: <u>Queen</u>
12. Spell: <u>Quick</u>

Answers

Spelling 2-11

1. Spell: <u>Summer</u>
2. Spell: <u>Winter</u>
3. Spell: <u>Any</u>
4. Spell: <u>Drawing</u>
5. Spell: <u>Many</u>
6. Spell: <u>Hide</u>
7. Spell: <u>Yellow</u>
8. Spell: <u>Away</u>
9. Spell: <u>Very</u>
10. Spell: <u>Head</u>
11. Spell: <u>Open</u>
12. Spell: <u>Show</u>

Spelling 2-12

1. Spell: <u>Stand</u>
2. Spell: <u>Bathe</u>
3. Spell: <u>Around</u>
4. Spell: <u>Think</u>
5. Spell: <u>Better</u>
6. Spell: <u>Asleep</u>
7. Spell: <u>Found</u>
8. Spell: <u>Clean</u>
9. Spell: <u>Full</u>
10. Spell: <u>Road</u>
11. Spell: <u>Story</u>
12. Spell: <u>Tuesday</u>

Answers

Spelling 2-13

1. Spell: <u>Park</u>
2. Spell: <u>Show</u>
3. Spell: <u>Pink</u>
4. Spell: <u>Wash</u>
5. Spell: <u>Skirt</u>
6. Spell: <u>Morning</u>
7. Spell: <u>Cloud</u>
8. Spell: <u>Ride</u>
9. Spell: <u>Horse</u>
10. Spell: <u>Anyone</u>
11. Spell: <u>Ever</u>
12. Spell: <u>Never</u>

Spelling 2-14

1. Spell: <u>Staring</u>
2. Spell: <u>Corner</u>
3. Spell: <u>Smoke</u>
4. Spell: <u>Butter</u>
5. Spell: <u>Spend</u>
6. Spell: <u>Sea</u>
7. Spell: <u>There</u>
8. Spell: <u>Awake</u>
9. Spell: <u>Yesterday</u>
10. Spell: <u>What</u>
11. Spell: <u>Your</u>
12. Spell: <u>Wednesday</u>

Answers

Spelling 2-15

1. Spell: <u>Truck</u>
2. Spell: <u>Dirty</u>
3. Spell: <u>Three</u>
4. Spell: <u>Name</u>
5. Spell: <u>Today</u>
6. Spell: <u>Cry</u>
7. Spell: <u>Walk</u>
8. Spell: <u>Very</u>
9. Spell: <u>Someone</u>
10. Spell: <u>His</u>
11. Spell: <u>Something</u>
12. Spell: <u>Thursday</u>

Spelling 2-16

1. Spell: <u>Road</u>
2. Spell: <u>Along</u>
3. Spell: <u>Lined</u>
4. Spell: <u>Our</u>
5. Spell: <u>Out</u>
6. Spell: <u>Beach</u>
7. Spell: <u>Died</u>
8. Spell: <u>Year</u>
9. Spell: <u>Hear</u>
10. Spell: <u>Ride</u>
11. Spell: <u>End</u>
12. Spell: <u>Fix</u>

Answers

Spelling 2-17

1. Spell: <u>Name</u>
2. Spell: <u>For</u>
3. Spell: <u>Cross</u>
4. Spell: <u>White</u>
5. Spell: <u>Rope</u>
6. Spell: <u>Because</u>
7. Spell: <u>Beside</u>
8. Spell: <u>Rose</u>
9. Spell: <u>Air</u>
10. Spell: <u>Window</u>
11. Spell: <u>Summer</u>
12. Spell: <u>Mouse</u>

Spelling 2-18

1. Spell: <u>Father</u>
2. Spell: <u>Gone</u>
3. Spell: <u>Coming</u>
4. Spell: <u>Front</u>
5. Spell: <u>Cold</u>
6. Spell: <u>Now</u>
7. Spell: <u>Forget</u>
8. Spell: <u>Next</u>
9. Spell: <u>New</u>
10. Spell: <u>Pull</u>
11. Spell: <u>Afternoon</u>
12. Spell: <u>Day</u>

Answers

Spelling 2-19

1. Spell: <u>Christmas</u>
2. Spell: <u>Think</u>
3. Spell: <u>Water</u>
4. Spell: <u>Brother</u>
5. Spell: <u>Than</u>
6. Spell: <u>Foot</u>
7. Spell: <u>Chair</u>
8. Spell: <u>Flower</u>
9. Spell: <u>Lunch</u>
10. Spell: <u>Full</u>
11. Spell: <u>Their</u>
12. Spell: <u>Wool</u>

Spelling 2-20

1. Spell: <u>Live</u>
2. Spell: <u>Cost</u>
3. Spell: <u>Horse</u>
4. Spell: <u>Lost</u>
5. Spell: <u>Blow</u>
6. Spell: <u>Page</u>
7. Spell: <u>Gold</u>
8. Spell: <u>Letter</u>
9. Spell: <u>Brave</u>
10. Spell: <u>Could</u>
11. Spell: <u>Should</u>
12. Spell: <u>Would</u>

Answers

Spelling 2-21

1. Spell: Shirt
2. Spell: Another
3. Spell: Friday
4. Spell: Will
5. Spell: Creek
6. Spell: Class
7. Spell: Those
8. Spell: Short
9. Spell: Town
10. Spell: Shout
11. Spell: Spring
12. Spell: Letter

Spelling 2-22

1. Spell: White
2. Spell: Hide
3. Spell: Under
4. Spell: Sharp
5. Spell: Door
6. Spell: Nice
7. Spell: Mail
8. Spell: Monday
9. Spell: Each
10. Spell: Hear
11. Spell: Sweet
12. Spell: Those

Other Books You'll Love!

1. **Spelling one: An Interactive Vocabulary & Spelling** Workbook for 5-Year-Olds. (With Audiobook Lessons)

2. **Spelling Two: An Interactive Vocabulary & Spelling** Workbook for 6-Year-Olds. (With Audiobook Lessons)

3. **Spelling Three: An Interactive Vocabulary & Spelling** Workbook for 7-Year-Olds. (With Audiobook Lessons)

4. **Spelling Four: An Interactive Vocabulary & Spelling** Workbook for 8-Year-Olds. (With Audiobook Lessons)

5. **Spelling Five: An Interactive Vocabulary & Spelling** Workbook for 9-Year-Olds. (With Audiobook Lessons)

6. **Spelling Six: An Interactive Vocabulary & Spelling** Workbook for 10 & 11 Years Old. (With Audiobook Lessons)

7. **Spelling Seven: An Interactive Vocabulary & Spelling** Workbook for 12-14 Years-Old. (With Audiobook Lessons)

Other Books You'll Love!

8. Raising Boys in Today's Digital World:
Proven Positive Parenting Tips for Raising Respectful, Successful, and Confident Boys

9. Raising Girls in Today's Digital World:
Proven Positive Parenting Tips for Raising Respectful, Successful, and Confident Girls

10. Raising Kids in Today's Digital World:
Proven Positive Parenting Tips for Raising Respectful, Successful, and Confident Kids

11. The Child Development and Positive Parenting Master Class 2-in-1 Bundle:
Proven Methods for Raising Well-Behaved and Intelligent Children, with Accelerated Learning Methods

12. Parenting Teens in Today's Challenging World 2-in-1 Bundle: Proven Methods for Improving Teenager's Behaviour with Positive Parenting and Family Communication

13. Life Strategies for Teenagers:
Positive Parenting, Tips and Understanding Teens for Better Communication and a Happy Family

14. Parenting Teen Girls in Today's Challenging World:
Proven Methods for Improving Teenager's Behaviour with Whole Brain Training

Other Books You'll Love!

15. Parenting Teen Boys in Today's Challenging World:
Proven Methods for Improving Teenager's Behaviour with Whole Brain Training

16. 101 Tips For Helping With Your Child's Learning:
Proven Strategies for Accelerated Learning and Raising Smart Children Using Positive Parenting Skills

17. 101 Tips for Child Development:
Proven Methods for Raising Children and Improving Kids Behavior with Whole Brain Training

18. Financial Tips to Help Kids:
Proven Methods for Teaching Kids Money Management and Financial Responsibility

19. Healthy Habits for Kids:
Positive Parenting Tips for Fun Kids Exercises, Healthy Snacks, and Improved Kids Nutrition

20. Mini Habits for Happy Kids:
Proven Parenting Tips for Positive Discipline and Improving Kids' Behavior

21. Good Habits for Healthy Kids 2-in-1 Combo Pack:
Proven Positive Parenting Tips for Improving Kid's Fitness and Children's Behavior

22. Raising Teenagers to Choose Wisely:
Keeping your Teen Secure in a Big World

23. Tips for #CollegeLife:
Powerful College Advice for Excelling as a College Freshman

Other Books You'll Love!

24. **The Career Success Formula:**
Proven Career Development Advice and Finding Rewarding Employment for Young Adults and College Graduates

25. **The Motivated Young Adult's Guide to Career Success and Adulthood:**
Proven Tips for Becoming a Mature Adult, Starting a Rewarding Career, and Finding Life Balance

26. **Bedtime Stories for Kids:**
Short Funny Stories and poems Collection for Children and Toddlers

27. **Guide for Boarding School Life**

28. **The Fear of The Lord:**
How God's Honour Guarantees Your Peace

Audiobooks

Purchase the audio version of Spelling 1 separately to enhance your child's spelling practice with immersive listening.

Are available at the following retailers:

1. Kobo
https://www.kobo.com/us/en/audiobook/spelling-one

2. Google Store
https://play.google.com/store/audiobooks/details/Bukky_Ekine_Ogunlana_Spelling_One?id=AQAAAEAi4SuhGM

3. Libro
https://libro.fm/audiobooks/9798368929880

4. Storytel
https://www.storytel.com/se/sv/books/4028820

5. Scribd
https://www.scribd.com/audiobook/631546677/Spelling-One-An-Interactive-Vocabulary-and-Spelling-Workbook-for-5-Year-Olds-With-AudioBook-Lessons

6. Audiobooks
https://www.audiobooks.com/audiobook/spelling-one-an-interactive-vocabulary-and-spelling-workbook-for-5-year-olds-with-audiobook-lessons/674795

7. Barnes and Noble
https://www.barnesandnoble.com/w/spelling-one-bukky-ekine-ogunlana/1143208355

8. Spotify
https://open.spotify.com/show/3u5811rG2LFRokWB710ekX

And all other audiobook retailers!

Audiobooks

Purchase the audio version of Spelling 2 separately to enhance your child's spelling practice with immersive listening.

Are available at the following retailers:

1. Kobo
https://www.kobo.com/us/en/audiobook/spelling-two-2

2. Google Store
https://play.google.com/store/audiobooks/details/Bukky_Ekine_Ogunlana_Spelling_Two?id=AQAAAEAieyE7EM

3. Libro
https://libro.fm/audiobooks/9798368929880

4. Storytel
https://www.storytel.com/se/sv/books/4028820

5. Scribd
https://www.scribd.com/audiobook/637100295/Spelling-Two-An-Interactive-Vocabulary-and-Spelling-Workbook-for-6-Year-Olds-With-AudioBook-Lessons

6. Audiobooks
https://www.audiobooks.com/audiobook/spelling-two-an-interactive-vocabulary-and-spelling-workbook-for-6-year-olds-with-audiobook-lessons/680176

7. Barnes and Noble
https://www.barnesandnoble.com/w/spelling-two-bukky-ekine-ogunlana/1143328313

8. Spotify
https://open.spotify.com/show/5OA8LA8tMNMiHrwFxRiM60

9. Hoopladigital
https://www.hoopladigital.com/title/16158722

Facebook Community

I invite you to our Facebook community group to visit this link and simply click the join group.

https://www.facebook.com/groups/397683731371863

This is a private group where parents, teachers, and carers can learn, share tips, ask questions, and discuss and get valuable content about raising and parenting modern children.

It is a very supportive and encouraging group where valuable content, free resources, and exciting discussion about parenting are shared. You can use this to benefit from social media.

You will learn a lot from schoolteachers, experts, counselors, and new and experienced parents, and stay updated with our latest releases.

See you there!

Your Free Gift

Your Free Gift!

As a way of saying thank you for Your purchase, I have included a gift that you can download at

TCEC publishing .com

References

1. https://www.theseus.fi/bitstream/handle/10024/50239/Anttila_Marianna_Saikkonen_Pinja.pdf
2. https://www.researchgate.net/publication/28372104_Early_Reading_Development
3. https://www2.ed.gov/parents/academic/help/adolescence/adolescence.pdf
4. http://centerforchildwelfare.org/kb/prprouthome/Helping%20Your%20Children%20Navigate%20Their%20Teenage%20Years.pdf
5. https://www.childrensmn.org/images/family_resource_pdf/027121.pdf
6. https://educationnorthwest.org/sites/default/files/developing-empathy-in-children-and-youth.pdf
7. https://www.researchgate.net/publication/263227023_Family_Time_Activities_and_Adolescents'_Emotional_Well-being
8. http://www.delmarlearning.com/companions/content/1418019224/AdditionalSupport/box11.1.pdf
9. https://exeter.anglican.org/wp-content/uploads/2014/11/Listening-to-children-leaflet_NCB.pdf
10. https://www.researchgate.net/publication/312600262_Creative_Thinking_among_Preschool_Children

www.ingramcontent.com/pod-product-compliance
Lightning Source LLC
Chambersburg PA
CBHW050353120526
44590CB00015B/1670